EAT SMART

A BALANCED DIET

Louise Spilsbury

Raintree

WITHDRAWN

C155278555

www.raintreepublishers.co.uk
Visit our website to find out more information about Raintree books.

To order:
☎ Phone 0845 6044371
🖨 Fax +44 (0) 1865 312263
🖳 Email myorders@capstonepub.co.uk

Customers from outside the UK please telephone +44 1865 312262

Raintree is an imprint of Capstone Global Library Limited, a company incorporated in England and Wales having its registered office at 7 Pilgrim Street, London, EC4V 6LB – Registered company number: 6695582

"Raintree" is a registered trademark of Pearson Education Limited, under licence to Capstone Global Library Limited

Edited by Charlotte Guillain and Diyan Leake
Designed by Richard Parker and Manhattan Design
Illustrated by Ken Vail Graphic Design (p. 5) and Geoff Ward (p. 23)
Picture research by Hannah Taylor
Production by Alison Parsons
Originated by Dot Gradations Ltd
Printed and bound in China by CTPS

ISBN 978 0 431066 15 8 (hardback)
13 12 11 10 09
10 9 8 7 6 5 4 3 2 1

ISBN 978 0 431066 22 6 (paperback)
10 9 8 7 6 5 4 3 2 1
14 13 12 11 10

British Library Cataloguing in Publication Data
Spilsbury, Louise
  A balanced diet. - (Eat smart)
  613.2

A full catalogue record for this book is available from the British Library.

Acknowledgements
We would like to thank the following for permission to reproduce photographs: © Alamy pp. **5** (moodboard), **11** (Glen Allison), **20** (Jupiterimages/Polka Dot); © Corbis p. **13** (Veer/Fancy); © Getty Images pp. **16** (StockFood PR), **18** (Photographer's Choice/Barry Yee); © Masterfile p. **9** (Chad Johnston); © iStockphoto pp. **1–32** background images; © PA p. **7**; © Pearson Education Ltd/MM Studios pp. **8**, **10**, **14**, **24**, **25** top, **25** bottom, **26**, **27** top, **27** bottom, **29** top, **29** middle, **29** bottom; © Photolibrary pp. **12** (Imagesource), **15** (Donald Higgs), **17** (Digital Vision); © Science Photo Library pp. **6** (Ian Hooton), **21** (Cordelia Molloy); © StockFood.com p. **4** (Maximillian Stock Ltd).

Cover photograph reproduced with permission of © Photolibrary (Westend61).

Every effort has been made to contact copyright holders of material reproduced in this book. Any omissions will be rectified in subsequent printings if notice is given to the publishers.

CONTENTS

Some words are shown in bold, **like this**. You can find out what they mean by looking in the glossary.

WHAT IS A HEALTHY DIET?

A healthy diet means eating a variety of different foods that together supply you with a balance of all the different **nutrients** you need. Nutrients are substances in food that supply you with **energy** and with raw materials for growth.

What are the different food groups?

The foods people eat can be divided into different groups: fruit and vegetables, grains, meat and **proteins**, milk and dairy, **fats** and oils. Grains are seeds such as rice and wheat. Meat and proteins include meat, fish, and eggs, and plant proteins such as lentils and chick peas. Dairy foods include milk and foods made from milk, such as cheese and yogurt. Fatty foods include butter and oil.

 The key to a balanced diet is variety. Eat smart by choosing a range of foods from the different food groups.

Why is it smart to eat a balanced diet?

To get a balance of the different nutrients you need, try to eat the right amounts of food from each group. You should eat mostly grains, fruit, and vegetables. You should eat some protein foods and some milk and dairy foods. You should limit the amount of foods you eat that are high in fat, as these can make you overweight and unhealthy. You should also drink lots of water.

Food gives you the energy you need to be active and stay well.

What not to do

To be healthy, there are also some things you should not take into your body. Smoking, drinking alcohol, and taking drugs affect the way the body functions. These effects can be harmful and dangerous, especially in a growing body.

WHAT NUTRIENTS DO FOODS GIVE YOU?

How do grains keep you healthy?

Grains are the body's main source of **carbohydrates**. The body breaks down carbohydrates into sugars that it uses for energy. Grain foods such as bread, pasta, or breakfast cereals are mostly made of **starches**. Starches can be broken down in the body into sugars. The body uses these sugars as fuel to drive all body processes.

Grains contain other nutrients, too. These include:

- **minerals** such as magnesium, which helps the muscles and heart work properly, and iron, which helps **oxygen** move throughout the body
- **vitamin** B6, which helps the body maintain a healthy brain and **nervous system**
- folic acid, which helps the heart work better
- **fibre**, which helps fill you up and keeps your **digestive system** healthy.

A breakfast with carbohydrate-rich grains such as oats and fruit such as raspberries supplies energy for the day ahead.

What grains should you eat?

A healthy diet includes three to five servings of carbohydrate each day. A single serving is equivalent to one slice of bread or six tablespoons of pasta or cereal. Try to make about half of your daily grains **wholegrains** rather than **refined**. Wholegrain foods include wholewheat bread and brown rice. Refined grains, such as white bread and white pasta, are made from grains with their outer skin (bran) and inner part (germ) removed. The bran contains most of the fibre and the germ contains many of the minerals and vitamins.

Other carbohydrates

Grains supply most of the starchy carbohydrates you need. Others come from vegetables and fruit. Vegetable carbohydrates include potatoes, yams, cassava, and sweet potatoes. Fruits packed with carbohydrates include bananas and apples.

Starch from grains is easy to digest and releases energy gradually and over a long time. This is ideal for long-distance athletes.

Fruit nutrients

There is a wide range of fruit products, from fresh and frozen to tinned and dried fruit. Fruit is rich in fibre, vitamins, and minerals. For example, oranges, kiwi fruit, and strawberries contain lots of vitamin C. This vitamin is important for healing cuts and wounds and keeping teeth and gums healthy. Bananas and prunes are rich in the mineral potassium. This helps keep your heart beating properly.

It is important to eat a variety of different types and colours of fruit to get a range of vitamins and minerals. Fruit is also low in fat and packed with fibre, which fills you up and makes you less likely to reach for unhealthy snacks.

Fruit juice facts

Fruit juices are considered to be a part of the fruit group. However, when fruit is **processed** to make juice, it loses some of the minerals and vitamins and all of the fibre that a whole piece of fruit may have. It is better to limit your fruit juice intake and eat whole fruits that are fresh, canned (in light syrup or juice), or dried.

Pick your vegetables

Vegetables are a good source of important vitamins, as well as fibre and other **nutrients** such as minerals. Choose a variety of vegetables to get more nutrients. Dark green and orange or red vegetables such as spinach, carrots, peppers, and tomatoes are also packed with antioxidants. These are substances that can help prevent diseases such as heart disease and cancer.

For a healthy snack, try crunchy carrot and celery sticks dipped in yogurt flavoured with fresh herbs such as parsley or basil.

How much should you eat?

Try to eat at least five portions of different fruit and vegetables a day. One portion of fruit or vegetables weighs about 80 grams (3 oz). This works out at roughly three tablespoons of chopped vegetables (raw, cooked, frozen, or tinned). A fruit portion is roughly equivalent to:

- one apple, banana, or similar sized fruit
- two plums or medium-sized fruits
- three tablespoons of fruit salad
- one heaped tablespoon of dried fruit (such as raisins)
- one handful of grapes.

Milk and dairy foods

Milk and dairy foods such as yogurt and cheese are a vital source of **calcium**. Calcium is a nutrient the body uses to build and maintain healthy bones and teeth. You can get calcium from other food sources, such as green vegetables and **pulses**, but it is easier to absorb calcium from dairy foods. Milk and dairy foods also contain **protein** and some vitamins.

Choosing dairy products

Cream, cream cheese, and butter are very high in **fat** and low in calcium. Eat these only in small amounts.

 You should try to eat three servings of milk and dairy foods each day. One glass of milk, one pot of yogurt or fromage frais, or one piece of cheese the size of a matchbox each amounts to one serving of dairy food.

Meat and protein

People get protein from meat, fish, eggs, nuts, beans, peas, lentils, and pulses. Proteins supply the raw materials your body needs for growth and repair. You should eat three servings of protein every day. The following each amount to one serving of protein: one egg; 55 grams (2 ounces) of cooked beef, chicken, or fish; eight tablespoons of lentils or beans; or one tablespoon of peanut butter.

Some protein foods contain a lot of fat. Eating too much fat is unhealthy. Meats such as pork and beef usually contain more fat than chicken, turkey, white fish, and seafood. Protein foods with the lowest fat levels are beans and pulses. These are also good sources of fibre.

Fish is a major source of protein worldwide.

Added extras

Most protein sources also supply other nutrients, such as B vitamins and the minerals iron and zinc. B vitamins help your nerves work properly, while your body needs iron to make blood. Zinc is essential for a healthy **immune system**, to fight infections.

WHY SHOULD YOU DRINK WATER?

Water is not a **nutrient**, but it is a vital part of a healthy diet. People can survive for weeks without eating food if they have to, but they would last only for a few days without water.

Water and the body

About two-thirds of the weight of a human body is made up of water. There is water in almost every part of your body – in your blood, skin, bones, and muscles. Water is also vital for keeping food moving through your stomach and other parts of the **digestive system**.

The amount of water you need depends on your age, your weight, how much physical activity you do, and what the temperature is like. You will need to drink more in the summer when it is hot, or if you are playing a match or going for a long bike ride.

How much should you drink?

You lose water regularly through sweat and **urination**, and as you cannot store water it is important to replace that supply every day. You should aim to drink at least six to eight large glasses of water per day. Try to drink one glass every hour or two. The colour of your urine shows whether you should be drinking more – if it is dark yellow then you need to drink more, since your urine should be pale and clear.

Fresh fruit and vegetables contain a lot of water so you can get some of the water you need from eating these foods.

Dehydration dangers

If people do not drink enough water they become dehydrated. This means the body is low on water. If you become thirsty you are already dehydrated. A small amount of dehydration makes people feel tired and moody and they may find it hard to concentrate. So don't wait until you feel thirsty – make sure you drink water throughout the day.

ARE FAT AND SUGAR BAD FOR YOU?

Chicken is healthiest when cooked in little or no oil, and with its fatty skin removed.

A small amount of **fat** is good for you – you need some fat in your diet because it helps your body work properly. Most fats come from animal sources, such as butter from milk. Many oils that come from plants, such as oil squeezed from olives or pressed from sunflower seeds, are also a source of fat.

Your body stores some fat from foods as body fat. This is a concentrated store of **energy** you can use when you do not have enough food to eat. The layer of fat stored around the body also helps keep you warm and cushions your delicate internal body parts from being damaged if you get bumped or knocked.

Types of fat

There are two types of fat: unsaturated and saturated. **Unsaturated fat** is better for your health. Vegetable oils are the main source of unsaturated fat. They contain fatty acids that are necessary for health and are also a major source of vitamin E. **Saturated fats** are found in butter, some margarines, lard, and the white fat in and around meat. They are commonly used to make cakes, pastries, and fried foods. Saturated fats can build up in your blood vessels and create heart problems.

◀ About 80 percent of the fat in peanut butter is unsaturated.

How much fat and oil?

While you need to consume some oil and fat to be healthy, you should limit the amount you eat because storing too much fat in the body makes people overweight. Try to eat no more than three to six teaspoonfuls a day and make most of this unsaturated fat. Limit saturated fats as much as you can, for example by putting just a thin layer of butter on bread and cutting white fat off meat.

Sugars

Sweet foods are a concentrated source of sugar which your body uses to produce energy. The body digests jam, sweets, chocolate, and soft drinks fast so the energy comes in a short burst. This is less useful than the longer, slower release of energy from starchy **carbohydrates**. Also, unlike starchy carbohydrate foods, sugary foods provide few other useful **nutrients**. In addition, any sugars not used up as energy convert into body fat. That is why eating sweet foods as more than an occasional treat often makes people overweight.

 People who like a sweet taste can include more naturally sweet foods, such as dried fruit, in their meals.

Sweet tooth

Sugar is also bad for teeth. When you eat sweet foods, the sugars inside them coat your teeth. **Bacteria** in your mouth then form a thin, hard layer called **plaque**, under which sugars change into acids. Acids are strong substances that wear away teeth. That is why you should eat only small amounts of sugary foods and clean your teeth twice a day.

Check labels on foods. Choose foods with less added salt and lower levels of fat and sugar.

What is wrong with junk food?

Junk foods are **processed** foods such as chocolate, chips, and burgers that are usually high in fat, sugar, or salt and contain few nutrients. These foods are not necessarily bad for you, so long as you eat them only once in a while and do not eat them instead of healthy alternatives such as fruit and vegetables.

How much salt should you eat?

Your body needs some salt to function well, but eating too much salt is unhealthy and can cause problems with **blood pressure**. You should try to eat no more than one teaspoon of salt a day. Processed foods such as baked beans, pizza, sausages, and burgers can contain a fairly high amount of salt, so limit the amount you eat and try not to add salt to food. Cut down on salty snacks such as crisps and packets of salted nuts, or look for low-salt alternatives.

HOW DOES THE BODY USE FOOD?

The body cannot use the food you take into your mouth as it is. To release and use the **nutrients** in food, the body must first digest (break down) the food.

Steps in digestion

First, **saliva** in the mouth softens the food and the teeth chew it up. When you swallow food, it passes down into the stomach. Food stays in the stomach for about five hours, where it is churned about with stomach acids. The acids break the food down into smaller and smaller pieces. From the stomach, the pieces of food move into the small intestine, where the pieces of nutrients become small enough to pass into the blood.

Teeth begin the process of digestion by crushing, grinding, and chewing the food into smaller pieces.

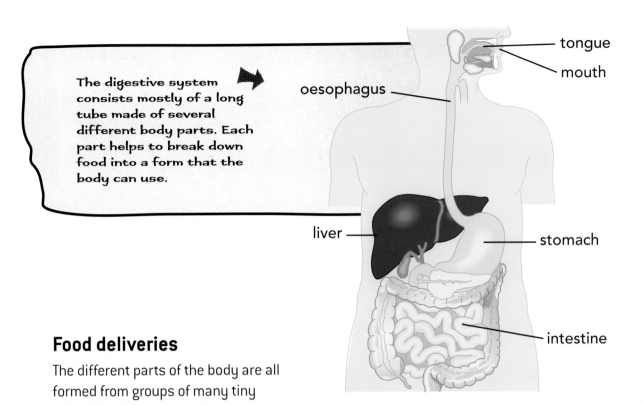

The digestive system consists mostly of a long tube made of several different body parts. Each part helps to break down food into a form that the body can use.

tongue

mouth

oesophagus

liver

stomach

intestine

Food deliveries

The different parts of the body are all formed from groups of many tiny **cells**. The blood carries the nutrients around the body to individual cells. The cells use the different nutrients in different ways. **Carbohydrate** sugars are mixed with **oxygen**, a gas in the air which you breathe in, to release **energy**. **Proteins** are used to build new cells and to repair damaged ones.

Getting rid of waste

Unwanted parts of food, such as **fibre** and other food waste, pass from the small intestine to the large intestine. Waste stays here for up to 24 hours while most of the remaining water is removed, and it gradually forms **faeces** (stools) which then pass out of the body.

What are friendly bacteria?

Bacteria are tiny living things. Some bacteria are known as "friendly" because they help digest food and keep parts of the **digestive system** healthy. These friendly bacteria also help to prevent the growth of harmful bacteria.

What are kilojoules?

Kilojoules are a unit of measurement that tells you the amount of energy the body takes from different foods. Kilojoules can come from fat, protein, or carbohydrate foods. You need to eat a certain number of kilojoules to stay alive and to provide the fuel you need for physical activity. The amount of kilojoules people need varies between males and females, and depends on a person's age and the amount of physical activity they do.

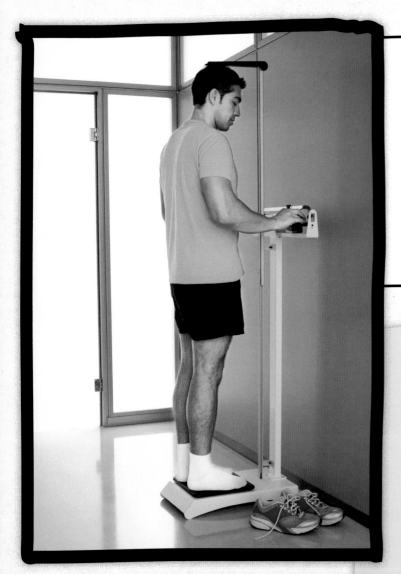

 The amount of kilojoules (kJ) you need depends on how active you are. A hard-working builder may need 20,000 kJ a day to stay at the same weight. An office worker who does not exercise may only need 6,000 kJ a day.

More or less?

If you take in more energy than you use, you will put on weight. This is because the body stores the extra kilojoules as body **fat**. If you consume fewer kilojoules than you use, you will lose weight.

Wholegrain foods, fruit, and vegetables provide lots of fibre and keep you feeling full for longer.

How does fibre help?

Fibre comes from plant foods. There are two types of fibre: **insoluble** and **soluble**. Soluble fibre can be partly digested by the body, whereas insoluble fibre cannot. Soluble fibre may help to reduce the amount of **cholesterol** in the blood. Cholesterol is a fatty substance that can cause fat to accumulate in people's arteries (blood vessels) if they eat too many fatty foods. Oats, beans, and lentils are particularly good sources of soluble fibre.

Insoluble fibre

Insoluble fibre is fibre the body cannot digest. This fibre passes through the parts of the digestive system without being broken down, but as it does so it helps food and waste products move through the intestines more easily. This keeps the large intestine healthy and stops **constipation**. Foods rich in insoluble fibre include **wholegrain** bread, brown rice, wholegrain pasta, oats, beans, peas, lentils, seeds, fruit, and vegetables.

HOW MUCH SHOULD YOU EAT?

It is important to eat a balanced diet to ensure you take in the full range of **nutrients** that your body needs. You also need to balance the amount of food you eat with the amount of **energy** you use up. When energy intake equals energy needs, your body is in "energy balance".

Balancing energy needs

Look at the two graphs opposite. The first shows how many **kilojoules** (kJ) of energy there are in different foods. To work out how many kilojoules are in a lunch, for example, you can add together a set of foods, such as a cheese sandwich, a bag of crisps, and an apple – 1879 kJ. The second graph shows how much extra energy you burn every minute during different activities. To find out how many extra kilojoules you burn in a day during exercise, multiply the activity measurement by the number of minutes you spend doing it.

Energy endorphins

Being physically active not only helps you burn up kilojoules, it also makes you happy. Physical activity makes your body release endorphins. These are natural body chemicals that make you feel good!

How much physical activity should you do?

There is no need to worry about working out your energy intake and output all the time. All you need to do to be healthy is eat a balanced diet and get lots of exercise. You can include physical activities such as football, dancing, swimming, and running, as well as walking to school or helping with household chores such as vacuuming the carpet. You do not have to do the 60 minutes all at once but can spread this out throughout the day.

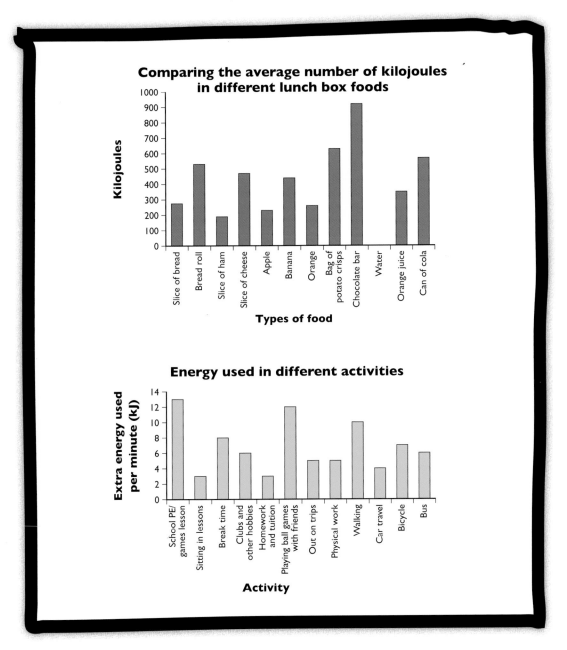

Comparing the average number of kilojoules in different lunch box foods

Kilojoules (y-axis, 0 to 1000)

Types of food (x-axis): Slice of bread, Bread roll, Slice of ham, Slice of cheese, Apple, Banana, Orange, Bag of potato crisps, Chocolate bar, Water, Orange juice, Can of cola

Energy used in different activities

Extra energy used per minute (kJ) (y-axis, 0 to 14)

Activity (x-axis): School PE/games lesson, Sitting in lessons, Break time, Clubs and other hobbies, Homework and tuition, Playing ball games with friends, Out on trips, Physical work, Walking, Car travel, Bicycle, Bus

Recipes for a balanced diet

Mexican quesadillas

These Mexican quesadillas make a balanced meal as they contain dairy food, **protein**, vegetables, grains, and some fruit juice!

Ingredients

- 100 g (4oz) Cheddar cheese
- 2 large tomatoes
- 1 small avocado
- 3 spring onions
- A squeeze of lemon juice
- Salt and pepper
- Vegetable oil
- 4 soft flour tortillas

Equipment

- Bowls
- Grater
- Knife
- Chopping board
- Lemon squeezer (optional)
- Frying pan

WHAT YOU DO

1 Grate the cheese into a bowl.

2 Wash the tomatoes and chop them into small pieces. Peel the avocado, discard the stone inside, and chop the flesh up and put it into a bowl with the tomatoes.

3 Cut off the roots and shoots from the spring onions and discard them. Chop the spring onions finely and add them to the tomato and avocado mixture. Add a squeeze of lemon juice and a little salt and pepper to this sauce, or "salsa".

4 Heat a little oil in the pan. Put in one of the tortillas and then about a quarter of the cheese on top. Heat this through for a few minutes.

5 Sprinkle 2 tablespoons of the tomato and avocado salsa onto one half of the tortilla.

6 Fold the tortilla in half. Cook for 30 seconds and then flip the tortilla over. Cook this side for 30 seconds and then put the cooked tortilla onto a plate. (You could keep this warm in the oven while you prepare the other tortillas.)

7 Cook the remaining tortillas in the same way. Serve the tortillas cut into two or three pieces.

Spinach omelette

If you serve this omelette with a salad and slice of bread, it makes a very healthy meal – especially if you follow it with a piece of fruit and a glass of milk or water!

Ingredients

- 2 spring onions
- 1 leek
- 40 g (1½ oz) fresh spinach leaves
- 1 sprig parsley
- 1 tablespoon fresh oregano
- 1 tablespoon fresh thyme
- 6 large eggs
- Salt and pepper
- 25 g (1 oz) butter

Equipment

- Knife
- Chopping board
- Mixing bowl
- Fork
- Ovenproof dish
  (about 20 cm or 8 in. across)
- Baking foil

WHAT YOU DO

1 Preheat the oven to 170 °C/ 325 °F/gas mark 3.

2 Wash and dry all the vegetables.

3 Cut off the roots and shoots from the leek and the spring onions. Chop the leek and spring onions into small pieces.

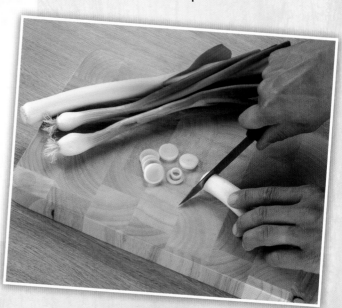

Always ask an adult to help you in the kitchen.

4 Chop the spinach and herbs finely, too.

5 Break the eggs into the mixing bowl and use a fork to mix the eggs together. Then put the chopped vegetables and herbs in with the egg mixture.

6 Grease an ovenproof dish with the butter. To do this, take a small piece of greaseproof paper or a butter wrapper and spread a thin layer of butter over the inside of the dish.

7 Pour the omelette mixture into the dish. Put a piece of baking foil over the top and place the dish into the oven for 30 minutes.

8 Carefully remove the foil and then bake the omelette for another 10 minutes, to brown the top.

Bean and egg salad

When served with a **carbohydrate** such as crusty **whole-grain** bread, this recipe makes a balanced meal because it also includes vegetables, and beans and eggs for protein.

Ingredients

- 1 red onion
- 2 tablespoons olive oil
- 1 tablespoon balsamic vinegar or red wine vinegar
- 1 tablespoon mayonnaise
- 200 g (8 oz) canned kidney bean
- 200 g (8 oz) canned haricot beans
- 300 g (12 oz) green beans
- 2 or 3 large lettuce leaves
- 2 eggs

Equipment

- Knife
- Chopping board
- Mixing bowl
- Saucepan
- Colander
- Spoon
- Serving plate

WHAT YOU DO

1 In a bowl, mix together the oil, vinegar, and mayonnaise.

2 Peel the onion and finely chop it.

3 Drain the kidney and haricot beans and add them and the chopped onion to the bowl.

4 Cut the ends off the green beans. If they are long, cut them in half.

5 Boil water in a saucepan and add the green beans to the pan. Boil the beans for 5 minutes, then drain the water from the beans in the colander (over a sink) and leave the beans to cool.

6 Use the spoon to gently place the eggs in a saucepan. Cover them with water. Bring the water to the boil, then reduce the heat and simmer the eggs for 8 minutes.

7 Use the spoon to lift the eggs out of the water. Hold them under a cold tap to cool them, then peel off the shells.

8 Arrange the lettuce leaves on a plate. Put the kidney and haricot bean mixture in the middle of the lettuce leaves.

9 Arrange the green beans in a circle around the bean mixture. Cut the eggs into slices and arrange these around the green beans.

GLOSSARY

bacteria extremely small organisms that can only be seen using a microscope. Some bacteria can cause disease or sickness.

blood pressure force exerted by the heart in pumping blood around the body

calcium mineral used by the body to help maintain bones and teeth. Calcium also has an important role in muscle contraction, blood clotting, and nerve function.

carbohydrate type of nutrient found in food. The body breaks down carbohydrates into sugars that it uses for energy.

cell all living things are made up of millions of microscopic parts called cells. Different parts of the body are made up of different types of cells.

cholesterol fatty substance found in all parts of the body. The body makes some cholesterol and people also eat some cholesterol in food products from animals. Excessive cholesterol can block arteries and lead to heart disease.

constipation condition in which food moves very slowly through the digestive system and forms hard, dry stools that are uncomfortable to pass out of the body

digestive system stomach, intestine, and other body parts that work together to break down food into pieces so small they dissolve in liquid and pass into the blood

energy people require energy to be active and to carry out all body processes, including breathing

faeces stools, or the solid waste that you pass out of the body when you go to the lavatory

fat one of the nutrients that gives you energy. The body uses only a small amount of fat, so eating too much can make people overweight.

fibre part of food that cannot be digested but helps to keep the bowels working regularly

immune system the human body's system of defences against disease. The immune system includes white blood cells and antibodies that react against bacteria and other harmful material.

insoluble cannot be dissolved in liquid

kilojoule unit of measurement that tells you the amount of energy the body gets from different foods

mineral substance that comes from non-living sources, such as rocks that break down and become part of the soil. Some of the nutrients that plants take in through their roots are minerals.

nervous system system of nerves that regulates and coordinates all the body's activities

nutrient substance found in food that is essential for life

oxygen a gas in the air

plaque a thin layer of bacteria, saliva, and food that sticks to teeth

processed prepared and changed from a natural state to make a new product, such as when milk is processed into cheese or meat is processed into sausages

protein nutrient that provides the raw materials the body needs to grow and repair itself

pulse edible seed that grows inside the pods of various plants

refined processed by machines that remove some natural substances from food, such as the bran and the germ from grains

saliva spit, or liquid in the mouth

saturated fat type of fat found in animal sources such as butter and meat. Saturated fats can build up in your blood vessels and create heart problems.

soluble can be dissolved in liquid

starch a plant's store of excess glucose (food)

unsaturated fat type of fat found in vegetable oils. Unsaturated fats contain fatty acids that are necessary for health and are a major source of vitamin E.

urination passing liquid waste out of the body

vitamin nutrient people require to grow and stay healthy

wholegrain entire grain seed of a plant. Wholegrains contain more nutrients and fibre than refined grains, which have some of the grain seed removed.

FIND OUT MORE

At **www.eatwell.gov.uk** there is a wide range of information including tips on eating healthy foods and keeping food safe.

The BBC website **www.bbc.co.uk/health/healthy_living/nutrition** covers many aspects of healthy eating.

At **www.childrenfirst.nhs.uk/teens/health/healthy_eating** there are sections on healthy eating and the digestive system, and a body mass index calculator to find out if you are a healthy weight.

At **kidshealth.org/kid** there is a large section on staying healthy and some recipes to try.

Click on the "Healthy eating' link at **www.nutrition.org.uk** for ideas for healthier lunches, a closer look at the Eatwell plate, and more.

At **www.energyquest.ca.gov/projects/peanut.html** there is an explanation of an experiment you can try that uses the energy (kilojoules) in peanuts to heat water!

INDEX